Accounting

Financial Accounting, Accounting Principles, and Management Accounting

By

Income Mastery

TABLE OF CONTENTS

Introduction

Has it ever happened to you that you need the money and go to the petty cash of your company and never have? Or do you need resources and the company has no capital at the time?

This phenomenon is repeated a lot in companies that do not have a serious team or dedicated to the accounting of the company, so there is no control of the budget of the same.

But do you know what accounting means?

It is an area belonging to public accounting whose objective is the chronological recording of identifiable and quantifiable economic events. It is also the main tool for decision making, since it is based on the financial information generated by an entity, and its objective is to produce and communicate important information about the company's finances.

Accounting is also a great ally of the budget and allows you to have absolute control of the company's finances, preventing financial accidents from occurring in it, such as going into bankruptcy, having a capital flight, or avoiding massive expenses in the budgets.

Accountants are experts in managing a company's assets, which provide a sort of economic indicator of the status of the company's finances. These statuses are completely meticulous, which allows for the rapid identification of any flaws within the entire organization, because the larger the organization, the greater the level of care for the company's assets and finances must be. The accounting has many basic elements that must be taken into account when evaluating the patrimony of the company as patrimonial masses, structure of balances (active and passive), accounting books, among others, which will be developed throughout this text and explained in detail so that you can have an apt knowledge for the development of the accounting of your company or your income.

It is said that accounting and its various techniques are linked to the development of trade, agriculture and industrialization as activities of economic power, which was born in ancient Rome, because it was sought to keep the record of transactions and results obtained in all commercial activity of the time, and even speculates that accounting began when transactions were made through barter and that they were not liquidated at the time of delivering or receiving the goods.

Many archaeologists have found in the civilizations of the Inca Empire, Ancient Egypt and Rome, several manifestations of accounting records that, in a basic way, constitute a record of the entries and exits of marketed products, as well as of money. The use of currency was of paramount importance for the development of accounting because there was no room for such an evolution in a barter economy.

According to historians, and although there are few documents preserved from ancient Rome that verify the following information, it is known that accounting played a relevant role in the Roman economy, since the registration of loans in the creditor's accounting book (Codex ration) and the book of income and expenditure (codees acceti et expensi) were admitted as legal means of proof for that time.

Do you know the Double Split system?

It is the method or system of recording operations most used in accounting. Each operation is recorded twice, once in duty and once in credit, to establish a connection between the various elements of heritage. The annotation involving the two items (duty and credit) is called an accounting entry. This system is similar to a balance in equilibrium because, within an accounting entry, the sum of the concepts of duty and credit always has to be equal.

In the face of modern data processing systems, the convenience of separating the concepts active, passive and result in two columns is maintained, to convert the newspaper into support with computer quality.

Types of accounting

Accounting can be classified in two ways depending on the division criteria used. Depending on the type of business entity to which the generated accounting information refers, the following classification can be made:

- Accounting theory: it is made up of rules, norms, principles, techniques, procedures, criteria and instruments that are the basis of accounting.

- Accounting process: is a set of steps and procedures that are part of the development and fulfillment of the goals that an entity has, which are: systematization, valuation, processing, evaluation and finally the result in information.

Macro accounting

It refers to national accounts, as it provides a systematic numerical representation of a country's economic activity over a given period. It is prepared by States and provides useful information to guide the country's economic policy.

Micro accounting

It is the accounting of small economic units. Its main function is to provide information that will be used in decision-making. Within micro accounting, a distinction is made between public accounting, carried out by the different public administrations, and private accounting, oriented towards the company. In business accounting, users of accounting information can be divided into two: internal and external.

The group of internal users is made up of all those people or organizations that use the information from within the company to make appropriate decisions in the direction of the company. External users use accounting for the management of the company object of the information, and include all those entities that are not involved in the management, such as shareholders, creditors, lenders, customers, investors, employees and the public administration, especially the tax administration, and who basically need accounting information to also make decisions and control the company from multiple points of view.

Depending on the users or participants of the accounting, they are classified between financial accounting and management accounting:

- Financial accounting (external): provides essential information on the operation and financial status of the company to all interested economic agents (customers, investors, suppliers, public administrations, etc.). The legislation of many of the countries of the world regulates the norms and rules of financial accounting because in this way they seek to homogenize the resulting information and give it greater credibility and comparability. Financial accounting often has little detail because it contains very aggregated information.

- Management accounting or directive accounting (internal): it is the accounting elaborated with an internal purpose or of self-consumption in the own company, and it is used for the calculation of the costs, economic and productive states in the interior of the company that will serve to make decisions as for production, organization, marketing, etc. Its main characteristic is to be more flexible, as it is based on self-regulation. It is subject only to the rules imposed by the company itself and not to legal rules, since it is usually more detailed than financial accounting, and it is also more immediate than financial accounting because it has to be used for very close decisions. Cost accounting is a very useful tool for the internal use of company directors for the development of planning, control, and decision-making functions.

Basic concepts and accounting statements within the accounting structure

As we mentioned at the beginning, there are several terms and concepts that are part of accounting, and that you must consider when creating the accounting of your business. Right now, we're going to talk about some of them.

- Active: It is constructed by goods and services that have diverse functional and operative capacities that are maintained during the complete development of each socioeconomic activity. It should be noted that in the case of companies, their assets vary according to the nature of the activity carried out.

Asset Types

The different types of assets are as follows:

- Current assets: goods and rights acquired to remain less than one year, as is the case of stocks.

- Non-current assets or fixed assets: goods and rights acquired with the intention of remaining in the company for more than one year, which has not been acquired for sale purposes, such as machinery and real estate.

- Financial asset: the same intangible asset embodied insecurity or simply in an accounting notation, by which the buyer of the security acquires the right to receive future income from the seller. Financial assets are issued by economic units of expenditure and constitute a means of maintaining wealth for those who own them and liability for those who generate it.

- Intangible asset: the intangible asset is intangible in nature. For example, the value of a brand, which cannot be measured physically. It is considered in accounting because it can generate future economic benefits that can be controlled by the economic entity.

- Underlying asset: is subject to a standard contract and is the object of exchange, i.e. the asset on which a derivative asset is traded.

- Functional asset: the part of the asset that contributes, in accordance with the aims and objectives of a company, to the production of its goods and services.

- Deferred assets: represent costs and expenses that are not charged in the period in which the disbursement is made, but postponed to be charged in future periods, which will benefit from the income produced by these disbursements, applying the accounting principle of the association of income and expenses. These are expenses that do not occur recurrently.

- Long-term assets: these are tangible assets with an average life of more than one year, which are not made for resale and which are used in the operations of a business. These may include plant and equipment, but not inventory or accounts receivable. Those that have a physical appearance and can be touched, such as coins, buildings, real estate, vehicles, inventories, equipment, and precious metals.

- Short-term assets: are securities issued by public or private entities to obtain w/financial resources from investors. Financially speaking, these are outright transactions generally issued at a discount, consisting of a benefit (the cash delivered at the start of the transaction) and a consideration (the nominal amount of the security to be received at the end of the transaction).

Liabilities

This represents the debts and obligations with which a company finances its activity and serves to pay its assets. It is also known as financial structure, financial capital, the origin of resources and source of external financing.

They are debts that we have in the present but that we have contracted in the past. An example of an obligation is a loan with a financial institution. When you purchase that loan, you are required to pay the principal and interest to the supplier (documented on an invoice or bill of exchange).

Components of liabilities

- Non-current liabilities: this is composed of all those debts and financial obligations that a company has in the long term. In short, they are debts with a maturity of more than one year. As they expire in more than one year, they will not have to return the principal during the current year. Now, what you do have to pay is interest.

- Current liabilities: this is the part of the liability that contains a company's short-term obligations, i.e. debts and obligations that have a duration of less than one year. For this reason, it is also known as short term exigent.

The distinction between current and non-current liabilities is not found in their nature but rather based on the maturity date of the debt.

Degrees of enforceability of liabilities

The shortest or longest term was available to settle a debt or obligation.

- A higher degree of enforceability. Debt has a higher degree of enforceability, the shorter the period of time available to pay it off.

- A lesser degree of enforceability. Debt has a lower level of enforceability when the time available to pay it off is longer.

Depending on their greater and lesser degree of enforceability, the debts and obligations that form part of the Liability are classified into three groups:

Current or floating liabilities. This group is made up of all debts and obligations maturing in less than one year; the main characteristic of these debts and obligations is that they are in constant movement or rotation.

The main factors that form the current or floating liabilities are:

- Suppliers

- Notes payable

- Sundry creditors

Fixed or consolidated liabilities. It is made up of all debts and obligations maturing in more than one year, counted from the date of the Balance Sheet.

The main factors that make up the Fixed or Consolidated Liabilities are:

- Mortgages Payable or Mortgage Creditors

- Notes payable (long-term)

When there are long-term loans, say five years, of which a certain part must be covered monthly or annually, that part must be considered a Current Liability and the rest of the loan a Fixed or Consolidated Liability.

Deferred Liabilities or Deferred Credits. This consists of all the amounts collected in advance for which it is obligated to provide a service, both in the same year and in subsequent years.

The main services charged in advance that make up the deferred liability or deferred credits are as follows:

- Income collected in advance

- Interest charged in advance.

Amounts charged in advance should be considered a Liability because they generate the obligation to provide a service equivalent to the amount charged in advance.

Services or products charged in advance have as their main characteristic that their value decreases with the passing of time or as such services are provided.

For example, the advance payment of two years of rent with a value of $60,000.00 each, which was received at the beginning of the fiscal year, it is natural that at the end of the term the same amount will not be had since its value has been decreasing as time has passed.

If we evaluate this example, we can appreciate that, of the services charged in advance, only the part diminished by the passage of time should be considered useful and the rest, a deferred Liability.

It should not be forgotten that any service charged in advance is convertible into utility as time passes or services are provided.

Capital

Designates the difference between the assets and liabilities of a company. Presents the investment of owners or shareholders in an entity and consists of their plus or minus contributions retained earnings or accumulated losses, plus other types of surpluses such as the excess or insufficiency in the accumulation of stockholders' equity and donations.

Part of stockholders' equity:

- Capital stock.

- Contributions.

- Donations.

- Retained earnings due to being in the Reserve or due to pending application.

- Accumulated losses.

- Updating of Stockholders' Equity.

Composition of capital

It is composed of contributed capital and earned capital.

- Contributed Capital: Refers to contributions from owners and donations received by the entity. Within the Contributed Capital, we have the Social Capital.

- Share Capital: These are the contributions of partners or shareholders, considered in the articles of association or in their reforms. It is composed of:

- Unissued Authorized Capital: This is the difference between the capital of the company authorized in the deeds and the amount that has been put to subscription. This difference may or may not be subscribed, from the point of view of the Financial Statements it is not an integral part of the Accounting Capital, but it is an element of Information.

- Unsubscribed Issued Capital: It represents that part of the issued capital in the minutes of the shareholders' meeting and pending to subscribe, this part of the social capital is not an element of the stockholders' capital from the financial point of view, but from the informative point of view.

- Subscribed Capital: It represents the part of the issued capital that the partners or shareholders undertake to exhibit, from the point of view of the Financial Statements YES, it is an integral part of the Accounting Capital.

- Capital Subscribed and not exhibited: It is the Capital or patrimony Subscribed by the partners or shareholders whose money is pending to receive, it will have to be presented in the Statement of Financial Situation diminishing the Subscribed capital.

- Exhibited Capital: Represents the amount that the partners or shareholders have exhibited or have effectively contributed.

- Earned Capital: The result of the entity's activities and other influencing events or circumstances, such as the adjustment for recovery of changes in prices that have to be recognized.

Expenses (outgoings)

In accounting, expense or expenditure is the entry or accounting item that decreases the profit or increases the loss of a company or individual. It differs from the term cost because it specifies that there was or will be a financial outlay.

Expenditure is an exit of money that is "not recoverable", unlike cost, which it is, because the exit is with the intention of obtaining a profit, which makes it a recoverable investment: it is an exit of money and also obtains a profit.

We can also say that the expense is the flow of resources or potential services that are consumed in obtaining the net product of the entity: its income.

Expense is defined as the expiration of assets voluntarily incurred to produce income.

Income

These are the amounts that a company receives for the sale of its products or services, also, they are the set of income received by the citizens. This income is divided into:

Business income: increases in the net worth of the company during the financial year, either in the form of inflows or increases in the value of assets or decreases in liabilities, provided they do not originate from contributions, monetary or otherwise, by partners or owners. When income originates from productive activities, it can be classified as:

- Total income.

- Marginal income: generated by the increase in production by one unit.

- Average income: obtained, on average, for each unit of product sold; that is, it is the total income divided by the total number of units sold.

- Marginal product income: generated by the task of accounting for some factor of production, for example, the use of one more worker.

- Ordinary and extraordinary income: income can also be classified as ordinary and extraordinary.

    o Ordinary income is all income that is earned regularly. For example, the salary of a worker who is engaged in a stable job or the sales of a company or organization to a customer who acquires regularly or on a regular basis.

    o Extraordinary income is all that comes from special events. For example, an unexpected business by a person or a bond issue by a government.

Public income: States also receive income, called public income. The State receives, with the public budget, income from the collection of taxes, from the sale of goods produced by public companies, from the profits they generate, from sales or rentals of properties, from fines imposed or from the issuance of bonds or the obtaining of credits, among others. When the income is taxable, it is called taxable income, but when it comes from sources other than taxes, it is called non-taxable income. With this income, government agencies can make their expenditures, investments, etc.

Financial Statements

Financial statements, also called accounting statements, financial reports or annual accounts, are reports that are used by institutions to disclose the economic and financial situation and the changes that may occur at a given date or period. This information is very useful for the Administration, managers, regulators and other types of stakeholders such as shareholders, creditors or owners.

Most of these reports frame the final product of accounting and are prepared in accordance with generally accepted accounting principles, accounting standards or financial reporting standards. Accounting is carried out by public accountants who, in most countries of the world, must be registered with public or private auditing bodies to practice the profession.

The mandatory financial statements may depend on each country, and the most common components are the following:

- Statement of net worth, also known as Statement of Financial Position, Balance Sheet or Balance Sheet.

- The income statement is the Statement of Profit and Loss or profit and loss account.

- Statement of changes in equity, also known as the Statement of Changes in Equity.

- Cash flow statement.

- Memory, known as Notes to the Financial Statements.

- Non-financial information report, (mandatory in 2018).

The Financial Statements are of great importance for all users since they have data that, complemented with other information such as the conditions of the market in which it operates, allow to diagnose and evaluate all the policies to continue considering new trends (limitations of the financial statements). Likewise, it is said that for the presentation of the financial statements, real information should be considered to be more accurate with the results.

The financial information must collect or collect certain qualitative characteristics to provide the fulfillment of its objectives and, consequently, to ensure its efficient use by its different addressees (users).

The characteristics that the financial statements must have are:

1. Comprehensibility: refers to information or data that should be easily understood by all users, however, notes should also be added to allow understanding of complex issues, for decision making.

2. Relevance/systematization: information will be of relative importance if, when such information is presented and mistakenly omitted, it may prejudice and influence the decisions taken.

3. Reliability: all the information must be free of any material error, must be neutral and prudent so that it can be useful and transmit the necessary confidence to users.

4. Comparability: this information must be presented in accordance with accounting rules and policies so that it can be easily compared with previous periods to know the trend, and it will also allow comparison with other companies.

5. Belonging: Must meet users' needs.

GDP - Gross Domestic Product

It is a macroeconomic magnitude that expresses the monetary or patrimonial value of the production of goods and services of the final demand of a country or region during a determined period, normally one year or quarterly.

GDP is used as an object of study of macroeconomics. Some complementary approaches are used for their estimation. After the obligatory adjustment of the results obtained, partially, the black economy is included in its calculation.

However, there are limitations to its use, in addition to the above-mentioned adjustments needed for the black economy, the social or ecological impact of various activities may be important for what is being studied and may not be reflected in GDP. There are some alternative measures to GDP that may be useful for certain comparisons.

Variables Flow, Variables Fund, and GDP

GDP is a magnitude called flow that accounts only for goods produced or services provided during the study stage.

The true meaning of flow or current is contrasted with that of fund or stock. The first refers to a period (day, week, month, year, etc.), which must also be expressed clearly, although in many cases, given its diffusion and generalized use, this period can be understood. Thus, for example, a person's income is a current or flow, since the period in which it has been obtained must be explained. For this reason, the currents or flows have a clear temporal dimension. On the opposite side, some funds or stocks lack it, even if there is a reference to a point in time. A person's wealth or savings is a clear example of a variable fund.

Final production

GDP measures only final output and not so-called intermediate output, to avoid double counting. When reference is made to final goods and services, it means that goods produced in the period for use as raw material for the creation and manufacture of other goods and services should not be considered. Therefore, final goods and services include those produced in the period which, by their very nature, are not going to be integrated into any other production process, as well as those other goods which were not integrated into the production process at the end of the financial year, although they were intended for this purpose.

Valuation: Nominal GDP and Real GDP

Gross domestic product (GDP) is the total value of the flow of final goods and services. Since the Internal Product is an aggregate (total sum of numerous components), the units of measurement contained in it are heterogeneous (tons, kilowatt-hours, etc.). To obtain a total value, it is important to transform them into homogeneous terms, which is achieved by giving monetary values to the different goods and services. The Internal Product is the result of multiplication, in which two great factors participate: a real one, formed by physical units, goods, and services; another monetary one, integrated by its prices. Thus, it is concluded that a country would increase its Domestic Product by a percentage simply by having increased the general price level by the same percentage. To avoid the distortions or misinterpretations that this phenomenon causes in intertemporal comparisons, GDP is applied in real terms, which is not affected by changes in prices, since physical units are always valued based on prices in a base year. To find real GDP, the nominal GDP is divided by a price index known as the GDP deflator.

Nominal GDP: the monetary value of all goods and services produced by a country or economy at current prices in the year in which the goods are produced. By studying and evaluating the evolution of the Gross Domestic Product over time, at times of high inflation, a substantial increase in prices (even when production remains constant), can result in a significant increase in GDP, motivated exclusively by the increase in prices.

Real GDP: defined as the monetary value of all goods and services produced by a country or an economy valued at constant prices, i.e. according to the prices of the year taken as a basis or in comparisons. This calculation is carried out using the GDP deflator, according to the inflation index (or by computing the value of goods independently of the production year through the prices of a certain reference year).

Economic Growth

It is the growth of income or an increase in the value of final goods and services created by an economy (usually from a country or region) in a given period (usually in a year).

On a large scale, economic growth is the increase in certain indicators, such as the production of goods and services, increased energy consumption, savings, investment, a favorable trade balance, increased per capita calorie consumption, etc. The improvement of these indicators should theoretically lead to an increase in the living standards of the population.

How is economic growth measured?

Economic growth is usually measured as a percentage increase in real Gross Domestic Product or GDP; it is associated with productivity. Economic growth, thus defined, has been considered (historically) desirable, because it has a certain relationship with the number of material goods available and therefore a certain improvement in the level of people's quality of life; however, some specialists have pointed out that economic growth depends on GDP per capita, i.e. the income of a country's inhabitants.

Financial Accounting

It is the field of accounting that is responsible for summarizing, analyzing and reporting financial transactions belonging to a business. This involves the preparation of financial statements available for public consumption. Shareholders, suppliers, banks, employees, government agencies and business owners, among others, use this information to make decisions.

Financial accounting is governed by local and international accounting standards. Generally Accepted Accounting Principles (GAAP) are the standard framework of financial accounting guidelines used in any given jurisdiction. This includes the standards, conventions, and rules that accountants follow in recording, summarizing and preparing financial statements. On the other hand, the International Financial Reporting Standards (IFRS) are a set of accounting standards that state how certain transactions and other events should be reported on financial statements. With IFRS becoming more and more accepted on the international scene, consistency in financial reporting has become more prevalent among global organizations.

While financial accounting is often used to prepare accounting information for people outside the organization or not involved in the day-to-day running of the company, management accounting provides accounting information to help managers make better decisions or to run the business.

Financial accounting is the preparation of financial statements that can be consumed by anyone with an interest in a business using Historical Cost (HCA) or Constant Purchasing Power Accounting (CPPA). When making financial statements, the following must be met:

- Relevance: Financial accounting has to be specific in terms of decisions. In other words, it must be possible for accounting information to influence decisions. Unless this feature is present, there is no point in doing this process.

- Materiality: Information is material if its omission or error could influence the economic decisions of stakeholders based on financial statements.

- Reliability: The accounting must be free of risks or significant errors. Managers must be able to trust that what is stated is correct. Often, the highly relevant information is not very reliable, and vice versa.

- Understanding: Accounting reports have to be expressed as clearly as possible and have to be understood by those to whom the information is relevant.

- Comparability: Financial reports from different periods would have to be comparable to each other to draw meaningful conclusions about trends in an entity's financial position and performance over time. Comparability can be ensured by applying the same accounting policies.

Do you know the components of financial statements?

Cash flow statement

The cash flow statement considers the specific cash inflows and outflows within a stated period. The general template of a cash flow statement is as follows: Cash inflow - Cash outflow + Opening balance = Closing balance

Example 1: In early September, Ellen started with $5 in her bank account. During that month, Ellen borrowed $20 from Tom. At the end of the month, Ellen bought a pair of shoes for $7. Ellen's cash flow statement for September would look like this:

- Cash deposit: $20

- Cash Out: $7

- Initial balance: $5

- Bottom line: $20 - $7 + $5 = $18

Example 2: In early June, WikiTables, a company that buys and resells tables, sold 2 tables. They originally bought the tables for $25 each and sold them for $50 per table. The first table was paid in cash and the second was purchased on credit. The WikiTables cash flow statement for June would look like this:

- Cash Deposit: $50 - How much WikiTables received in cash for the first table? They did not receive cash for the second table (sold in credit terms).

- Cash Out: $50 - How much did you originally buy the 2 tables at?

- Initial balance: $0

- Final balance: $50 - 2*$25 + $0 = $50-50 = $0 - In fact, the cash flow for the month of June for WikiTables is $0 and not $50.

Important: The cash flow statement only considers the exchange of real money and ignores what the person in question owes or is owing.

Statement of income (Statement of income or statement of operations)

The income statement indicates changes in the value of a company's accounts during a given period (most commonly a fiscal year) and can compare changes in the same accounts during the previous period. All changes are summarized in the "bottom line" as net income, which is often referred to as a "net loss" when the income is less than zero.

The profit or loss is determined by:

Sales (income) - Cost of Goods Sold - Total Expenses + Total Income - Taxes Paid = Profit/Loss

- If the result is negative, it's a loss.

- If the result is positive, it's a benefit.

Balance sheet (Balance sheet)

The balance sheet is the financial statement that shows the assets, liabilities, and equity of a company on a specific date, usually, the end of the fiscal year reported in the corresponding income statement. Assets are equal to the sum of liabilities and their resources. Balance helps show the status of a company.

Accounting rules often establish a general format that companies must follow when presenting their balance sheets. Normally, IFRS requires companies to report current assets and liabilities separately from non-current amounts.

Current assets include:

- Cash - Physical money.

- Accounts Receivable - Income earned but not yet collected.

- Merchandise Inventory - Consists of goods and services that a company currently owns until it ends up being sold.

- Marketable securities - Stocks and bonds that a company has invested in other companies.

- Prepaid Expenses - Prepaid expenses for use during that year.

Non-current assets include fixed or non-current assets and intangible assets:

Fixed assets (long-term):

- Properties

- Buildings

- Equipment (such as machinery)

Intangible assets:

- Copyrights

- Registered Trademarks

- Patents

- Goodwill

Passive includes:

Current liabilities:

- Accounts payable

- Dividends payable

- Salaries of employees to be paid

- Interest (e.g. debt) payable

Long-term liabilities:

- Mortgage notes

- Bonds to be paid

Liabilities typically have the word "payable" on a balance sheet.

Own resources are represented differently depending on the type of business ownership. Business ownership can be in the form of a sole proprietorship, a business partnership or a corporation. For a corporation, the owner's resources are usually common stock and retained earnings (the income that was maintained in the company). Retained earnings come from the retained earnings statement, prepared before the balance sheet.

Important concepts to manage

The assumption of the stable currency unit: One of the basic principles in accounting is the assumption of the "stable currency unit":

"The unit of measurement in accounting will be the unit of money of the base of the most relevant currency. This assumption also assumes that the unit of measure is stable; that is, changes in its overall purchasing power are not considered important enough to require adjustments to the basic financial statements.

Historical Cost Accounting, the maintenance of financial capital in nominal monetary units, assumes of the stable monetary unit, under which accountants simply assume that money, the monetary unit of measurement, is perfectly stable in real value to measure:

- Monetary elements not cataloged by daily inflation in terms of daily CPI.

- Non-monetary items with constant real value not updated daily in daily CPI terms during inflation and low and high deflation.

Constant purchasing power units: The stable currency unit assumption is not applied during hyperinflation. IFRS requires entities to implement capital maintenance in units of constant purchasing power based on the IAS Financial Reporting in Hyperinflationary Economies.

Financial accountants produce financial statements based on accounting standards in a given jurisdiction. These standards may be the Generally Accepted Accounting Principles of a respective country, which are typically issued by a person charged with setting the standards at the national level, or the International

Financial Reporting Standards, which are issued by the International Accounting Standards Board.

Financial accounting has the following purposes:

- Produce general-purpose financial statements.

- Produce the information used by the management of a business entity to make decisions, make plans and make performance evaluations.

- Produce financial statements to meet regulatory requirements.

Financial Accounting Objectives

Systematic recording of transactions: the basic objective of accounting is systematically to record the financial aspects of business transactions ("doing the books"). The transactions recorded are later classified and summarized logically for the preparation of financial statements and their analysis and interpretation.

Verification of the results of recorded transactions: the accountant prepares profit and loss accounts to know the result of business operations for a particular period of time. If expenses exceed revenues, then the company is said to be running at a loss. Profit and loss accounts help management and investors - potential or current - make rational decisions. For example, if it cannot be proven that a business is remunerative or profitable, the cause of such status may be investigated by management to act.

Verification of the financial position of the company: businessmen are not only interested in knowing the result of the business in terms of profits or losses for a particular period, but also what they owe (liabilities) to others and what they own (assets) on a specific date. To know this, the accountant prepares a balance sheet on a particular date and assists in ascertaining the financial health of the business.

Providing information to users to make rational decisions: accounting as a 'business language' communicates a company's financial performance to various stakeholders through financial statements. Accounting is intended to cover the needs for financial information and assistance in making rational decisions.

Solvency position: in preparing the balance sheet, management not only discloses what the company has and owes but also gives information about its ability to pay its short-term (liquidity position) and also long-term (solvency position) liabilities, as well as how much is due and when it is due.

Accounting Principles

They are a set of rules, stipulations, and norms that function as an accounting guide to formulate criteria referred to the measurement of assets and the information of the patrimonial and economic elements of an entity. They form parameters so that the preparation of financial statements is based on uniform methods of accounting technique. These have as objective the uniformity in the presentation of the information in the financial statements, regardless of the nationality of who is reading and interpreting them.

It is composed of 14 principles

Principle of Equity

The principle of equity is synonymous with impartiality and justice and has the condition of basic postulate. It is an orientation guide with the sense of the ethical and fair, for the accounting evaluation of the facts that constitute the object of the accounting, and refers to the fact that the accounting information must be prepared with equity with respect to third parties and to the company itself, so that the financial statements reflect fairly the interests of the parties and that the information they provide is as fair as possible for the interested users, without favoring or disfavor someone in particular.

Entity Principle

The entity principle or entity principle establishes the assumption that the assets of the company are independent of the personal assets of the owner, considered as a third party. Separation is made between ownership (shareholders or partners or owner) and administration (management) as an indispensable procedure of accountability for the latter. The entity has a life of its own and is subject to rights and obligations, distinct from the persons who formed it.

The owners are creditors of the companies they have formed and although they have several companies, each one is treated as a separate entity, so the owner is one more creditor of the entity or company, which is accounting represented with the capital account.

Principle of Economic Goods

Financial statements always refer to economic goods, that is, material and immaterial goods that have an economic value and therefore can be evaluated in monetary terms.

Any asset, such as cash, merchandise, fixed assets in the power and/or use of the entity and over which the right is exercised, without necessarily being credited the property thereof, as long as it does not conflict with third parties that also claim the property, are subject to being recorded in regulatory books, through an adjustment entry, treatment that extends to the differences in acquisition costs or registration on a previous date.

Principle of Account Currency

Financial statements reflect equity through a resource that is used to reduce all of its heterogeneous components to an expression that allows them to be easily grouped and compared. It is a matter of choosing an account currency and valuing all the patrimonial elements applying a price to each unit. It is usually used as money that is legal tender in the country within which the "entity" operates and in this case the "price" must be given in units of legal tender.

In those cases where the currency used does not constitute a stable pattern of value, due to the fluctuations that it experiences, the validity of the principle that is sustained is not altered, for which reason the correction through the application of appropriate adjustment mechanisms is feasible.

Business as Usual Principle

This is an economic organism whose personal existence has full validity and future projection. This principle is also known as business continuity assumes that the company will continue its operations for an indefinite period of time and will not be liquidated in the foreseeable future, unless there are situations such as significant and continuous losses, insolvency, etc.

A start-up company or organization adds value to the resources it uses, establishing its profit by the difference between the sales value and the cost of the resources used to generate income, showing in the balance sheet the resources not consumed at their acquisition cost, and not at their current market value.

Principle of Valuation at Cost

The value of the cost (acquisition or production) is conformed by the main and basic criterion of valuation, which is conditional in the formulation of the financial statements called "situation", together with the concept of "going concern", which is why this standard acquires the character of principle.

This principle implies that the "market value" should not be adopted as a valuation criterion, understood as the "replacement or manufacturing cost". However, the "cost valuation" criterion linked to the "going concern" criterion, when the latter condition is interrupted or disappears, by this company in liquidation, including merger, the applicable criterion will be "market value" or "probable realization value", as the case may be.

Exercise Principle

The principle of exercise (period) means dividing the company's performance into uniform periods of time, to measure the results of management and establish the financial situation of the entity and comply with the legal and fiscal provisions established, particularly to determine income tax and the distribution of income. This periodic information is also of interest to third parties, such as banks and potential investors.

Accrual Principle

The meaning of accrual refers to recognizing and recording in accounts at a certain date, events or accounting transactions. In the application of the accrued term, income and expenses are recorded in the accounting period to which it refers, despite the fact that the supporting document was dated the following year or that the disbursement may be made in whole or in part in the following year. This principle eliminates the possibility of applying the perceived criterion for the attribution of results.

Principle of Objectivity

Changes that may occur in assets, liabilities and the accounting expression of equity should be formally recognized and highlighted in the accounting records as soon as they can be objectively measured and expressed in the currency of the account. Objectivity in accounting terms is evidence that supports the recording of equity variation.

Realization

The economic results should only be computed when they are carried out, that is, when the operation that originates them is perfected from the point of view of the applicable legislation or commercial practices and all the risks inherent to such operation have been fundamentally weighted. It must be established with a general character that the realized concept participates in the earned concept.

Principle of Prudence

Prudence means that when there is a choice between two values for an asset, normally the lower one should be chosen, or a transaction should be accounted for in such a way that the owner's share is lower. This general principle can also be expressed by saying: "account for all losses when known and only when gains have been enhanced".

Uniformity Principle

This accounting principle stipulates that, once the criteria for the application of the accounting principles have been drawn up, they must be maintained as long as the circumstances which led to their choice remain unchanged.

Principle of Materiality (Significance or Relative Importance)

When considering the correct application of general principles and particular rules, one must necessarily act in a practical sense. The principle of significance, which, also known as materiality, is guided by two fundamental aspects of accounting: Quantification or Measurement of Equity and Exposure of Financial Statement Items.

Principle of Exposure

This principle involves formulating all financial statements in a form that is understandable and understandable to users. It is directly related to the adequate presentation of the accounting items that group the balances of the accounts, for a correct interpretation of the recorded facts.

Classification of accounting

Accounting is classified according to the activities for which it is to be used. In other words, it is divided into two major sectors: Private and Official.

Types of Accounting

Public Accounting

It is a specialized branch of Accounting that allows developing the diverse processes of measurement, information, and control in the economic activity of the Public Administration. It is based on Public Accounting that the economic events in which public entities intervene are recorded in accounts, so that at all times you can know whether the status of rights and obligations, as well as the degree of collection of the various tax revenues, investments, cost and expenditure inherent in the economic process, made in the development of the administrative function or task.

In contrast to the public accountant, who serves many clients, in private industry the accountant is an employee of a single company. The head of the accounting department of a small or medium-sized enterprise is generally called a controller, in recognition of the fact that one of the primaries uses of accounting information is to help control the operations of the business. The comptroller must direct the work of the accounting department team, is part of the senior management team in charge of managing the business, establishing its objectives and ensuring compliance. The accountants of private companies, whether large or small, must record all transactions and prepare periodic financial statements from the accounting records.

Cost accounting

The branch of accounting responsibilities for the classification, accounting, distribution, collection of information on current and future costs.

- Included in the area of cost accounting are: the design and operation of cost systems and procedures; the determination of costs by departments, functions, responsibilities, activities, products, territories, periods and other units, as well as expected or estimated future costs and standard or desired costs, as well as historical costs; the comparison of costs from different periods; of actual costs with estimated, budgeted or standard costs; and alternative costs.

- The cost counter seeks to classify costs according to behavior patterns, activities and processes in which products are related to those that correspond and other categories, depending on the type of measurement desired. Having this information, the cost counter calculates, informs and analyzes the cost to perform different functions such as the operation of a process, the manufacture of a product and the realization of special projects. It also prepares reports that assist management in establishing plans and selecting courses of action. In general, the costs collected in the accounts serve three general purposes: To provide cost reports to measure the usefulness and to evaluate the inventory (income statement and balance sheet). Provide information for the administrative control of the company's operations and activities (control reports). Provide information to management to inform planning and decision making (analysis and special studies).

- Indeed, by being able to analyze, control and interpret the costs of production, distribution, administration and financing thanks to costing accounting, the calculation of the profit margin is much more accurate.

- Financial Accounting: refers to the obligation to present all financial statements for third parties such as shareholders, investments, public regulators, etc., and the need for the information presented or demonstrated to third parties to be uniform, which made accounting become the preparation of Financial Statements for third parties and not so much in collaborating in the preparation of information for corporate management. This objective of providing information to persons or entities outside the company is what mainly differentiates it from administrative accounting.

- Nowadays, due to the existing facilities as a consequence of the great computer advances, both the information for third parties and the information for the internal decision making of the company must come out of a single and integrated accounting system.

- It is a technique or formula used in the systematic and structural production of quantitative information expressed in monetary units of the transactions carried out by an economic entity and of certain identifiable and quantifiable economic events that affect it, in order to make it easier for the various interested parties to make decisions in relation to said economic entity. It shows the information provided to the general public, who are not involved in the management of the company, such as shareholders, creditors, customers, suppliers, trade unions and financial analysts, among others, although this information is also of great interest to the company's managers and directors. This accounting makes it possible to obtain information on the financial position of the company, its degree of liquidity and the profitability of the company.

- Tax accounting focuses on the tax criteria legally specified in each country, which defines how accounting should be carried out at the tax level. The importance of tax accounting for entrepreneurs and accountants is undeniable since it includes the registration and preparation of reports for the filing of returns and payment of taxes.

- Administrative accounting: Also called managerial accounting, designed or adapted to the needs of information and control at different administrative levels. It generally refers to the length of the internal reports, the design, and the presentation of which is currently the responsibility of the company's accountant. It is oriented to the administrative characteristics of the company and its reports do not leave the company, that is, its use is strictly internal and will be used by managers and owners to judge and evaluate the development of the entity on the policies, goals or objectives pre-established by the management or direction of the company; such reports will compare the past of the company, with the present and through the application of tools or control elements, foresee and plan the future of the entity.

- It can also provide any type of data on all the activities of the company, but usually focuses on analyzing the revenues and costs of each activity, the number of resources used, as well as the amount of work or depreciation of machinery, equipment or buildings. Accounting allows you to locate and obtain periodic information on the profitability of the different departments or areas of the company and the relationship between the forecasts made in the budget, also. can explain why there have been deviations. Administrative accounting is not regulated by rules or regulations as in financial accounting since its purpose is to serve senior management in the preparation of management reports for decision making.

- The administrative accounting is one that provides reports based on the accounting technique that helps the administration, the creation of policies for the planning and control of the functions of a company.

It deals with the quantitative comparison of what has been done with what has been planned, analyzing by areas of responsibility.

  o Activity-Based Accounting: A form of administrative accounting that involves the classification and operation of accounts for different activities, to facilitate the process of adjusting an organization's operations to a plan; function-based accounting. Its most important application is indicated in situations or times when planning, authority, responsibility, and accountability may be associated with small centers or units of operation. Because of its emphasis on responsibility for operations and accountability, activity-based accounting provides a greater reality as well as an incentive for delegation of administrative authority.

  o Service Organization Accounting: Applicable to all types of organizations and service industries and are defined in several ways. They are organizations that produce a service, rather than a tangible good such as public accounting firms, law firms, management consultants, real estate firms, transportation companies, banks, and hotels. Most non-profit or not-for-profit organizations are service industries. Examples: hospitals, schools, and a reforestation department.

    o   Managerial Accounting: this process requires data that are mandatory, such as who issues and receives invoices, item descriptions, quantities, unit and total costs of products or services, forms of payment (cash, transfer, check or unknown) to name a few. These records include the following: Inventories, Evaluation Methods, and Statements.

- These reports must be transformed into electronic files with the XML extension, encoded with the help of a computer system. In Mexico, as of July 1, 2014, legal entities, including nonprofit legal entities and individuals with business activity, are required to maintain electronic accounting and send this information to the SAT.

Conclusion

Accounting has many extensions. Among its main allies in the budget, savings, investment, and cost, all of which play a very important role in accounting. Many people are trained to understand and understand this science, because yes, this, like any area containing mathematics, is a very exact science, and must have a strict study of all the finances of a business, a family budget, and any enterprise.

The experts in accounting always see all the possible flanks before a situation or economic development of a company or organization, evaluating the costs, capital, assets, liabilities, patrimonies, miscellaneous expenses, and the financial fluctuation of the income and expenses of the organization. This always allows to maintain the stability of the company, it allows to know what is the economic scope that the organization has to spend or invest part of its capital, and thus to foresee any disaster or emergency that requires quick actions.

Accounting has different types and classifications, with two main ones, private and business, which were broken down and explained in detail during the development of this material. Although it is very necessary to have the support of an expert in accounting, you can manage them yourself at the beginning, understand how it works and take care of the economy of your venture, but as its capacity, quantity and structure increases, you should begin to consider the option of hiring an expert in this area, because you must avoid at all costs any financial risk that perhaps your eye can not detect, and that of an expert in the field yes.

Accounting does not only work in the private or business environment, but also in the governmental or organizational area, because in all the works, items or projects that an organization wishes to develop, it must have a meticulous accounting, in order to avoid the flight of capital, the fulfillment of the budgets in what has been established, to avoid thefts or incorrect repeal of these funds on the part of those in charge, or even to avoid the mafias and swindles on the part of the contractors. In the case of public works or those that are executed by the government of a country, one must be much more careful, because they are extremely large works and there are many people involved in them, starting with politicians or government chiefs, and even accountants are constantly audited to verify that they are fulfilling their job of accounting for the finances of the government cabinet.

There are 14 accounting principles, which must be respected and enforced for the proper development of a financial activity, and although we mentioned them in the book, here we highlight them:

1. Principle of Equity

2. Entity Principle

3. Principle of Economic Goods

4. Principle of Account Currency

5. Business as Usual Principle

6. Principle of Valuation at Cost

7. Exercise Principle

8. Accrual Principle

9. Principle of Objectivity

10. Realization

11. Principle of Prudence

12. Uniformity Principle:

13. Principle of Materiality (Significance or Relative Importance)

14. Principle of Exposure

To respect these principles assures a correct development within the accounting activity of a person or organization because they stick to the real facts of the different situations that can be presented in the economic, accounting and budgetary activity of a company. Even if you have the support of an accountant or expert in the accounting area, you must be trained in accounting, know the basic concepts, implementation plans and the operation of this subject, so that you can make a constant monitoring and auditing of the behavior of your company, as well as follow up every so often to ensure that everything is going in order.